CONTINENTS

Asia

Leila Merrell Foster

Heinemann
LIBRARY

www.heinemann.co.uk/library

Visit our website to find out more information about Heinemann Library books.

To order:
- ☎ Phone 44 (0) 1865 888066
- Send a fax to 44 (0) 1865 314091
- Visit the Heinemann Bookshop at www.heinemann.co.uk/library to browse our catalogue and order online.

First published in Great Britain by Heinemann Library, Halley Court, Jordan Hill, Oxford OX2 8EJ, part of Harcourt Education. Heinemann is a registered trademark of Harcourt Education Ltd.

Editorial: Kathy Peltan, Clare Lewis, and Katie Shepherd
Design: Joanna Hinton-Malivoire and Q2A Creative
Picture research: Erica Newbery
Production: Helen McCreath

Origination: Modern Age Repro House Ltd.
Printed and bound in China by South China Printing Co. Ltd.

13-digit ISBN 978-0-431-15811-2 (hardback)
10 09 08 07 06
10 9 8 7 6 5 4 3 2 1

13-digit ISBN 978-0-431-09893-7 (paperback)
11 10 09 08 07
10 9 8 7 6 5 4 3 2 1

British Library Cataloguing in Publication Data
Foster, Leila Merrell
Asia. – 2nd ed. – (Continents)
915
A full catalogue record for this book is available from the British Library.

Acknowledgements
The publishers would like to thank the following for permission to reproduce photographs: Tony Stone/Mike Surowiak p. **4**; Getty Images/Photographer's Choice/Stuart Dee p. **7**; Bruce Coleman Inc./J. Montgomery p. **9**; Bruce Coleman Inc./Burnett H. Moody p. **11**; Earth Scenes/Robert Kloepper p. **13**; Getty Images/Lonely Planet Images/Lee Foster p. **15**; Tony Stone/Mickey Gibson p. **16**; Bruce Coleman, Inc./M. Freeman p. **17**; Bruce Coleman Inc./Lynn M.Stone p. **18**; Bruce Coleman Inc./K&K Ammann p. **19**; Tony Stone/D.E. Cox p. **21**; Tony Stone/Orion Press p. **22**; Getty Images/Lonely Planet/Mark Daffey p. **24**; Bruce Coleman, Inc./Carolos V. Causo p. **25**; Tony Stone/Keren Su p. **27**; Corbis/Glen Allison p. **28**; Tony Stone/Chris Haigh p. **29**.

Cover photograph of Asia, reproduced with permission of Science Photo Library/ Worldsat International and J. Knighton.

The publishers would like to thank Kathy Peltan, Keith Lye, and Nancy Harris for their assistance in the preparation of this book.

Every effort has been made to contact copyright holders of any material reproduced in this book. Any omissions will be rectified in subsequent printings if notice is given to the publishers.

Some words are shown in bold, **like this**. You can find out what they mean by looking in the glossary.

Contents

Where is Asia?

There are seven continents. A continent is a very large area of land. Asia is the largest continent. The west of Asia is connected to the continent of Europe.

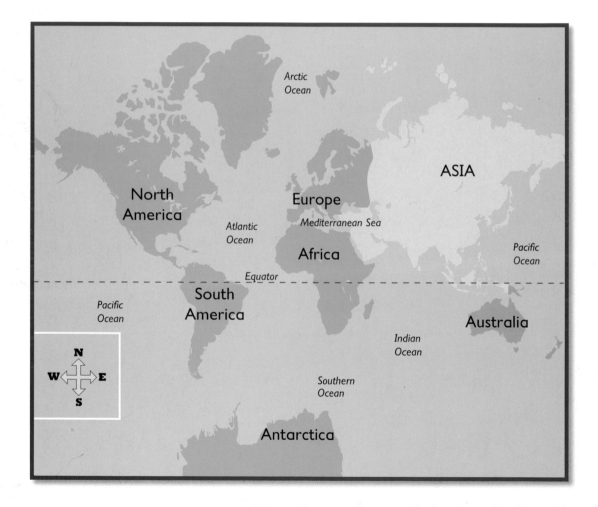

China is part of the Far East.

▲ *The island of Hong Kong, close to China*

The Mediterranean Sea is to the west of Asia. The Pacific Ocean is to the east of Asia. The countries on the Pacific coast are known as the Far East. The area around the Mediterranean Sea is part of the Middle East.

Weather

The countries of Asia have many different **climates**. Above the **Arctic Circle**, the land stays frozen all year round. In central Asia, there are vast **deserts**, where almost no rain falls.

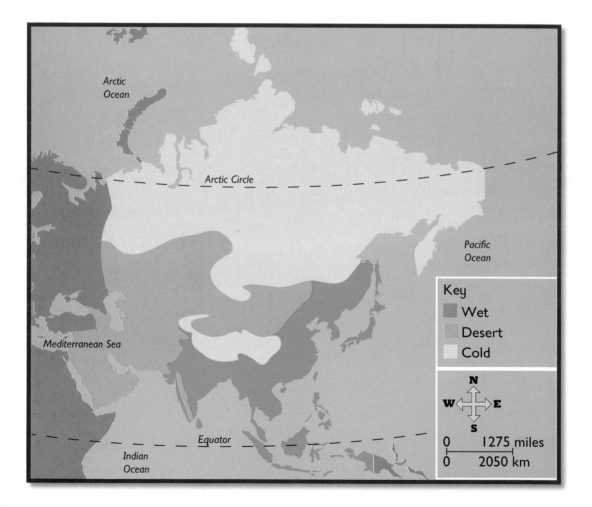

Arctic Ocean

Arctic Circle

Pacific Ocean

Mediterranean Sea

Equator

Indian Ocean

Key
Wet
Desert
Cold

N
W E
S

0   1275 miles
0   2050 km

▲ *Rainforest in Southeast Asia*

The **Equator** is an imaginary line around the centre of the Earth. Around the Equator, the weather is very hot. It rains every day in the **rainforests** of southern Asia. The weather is warm and sunny near the Mediterranean Sea.

Mountains

Asia has many high mountain **ranges**. There are also large areas of high, rocky land called plateaus. The Tibetan plateau is in southern China. It is higher than most mountains in Europe or the USA.

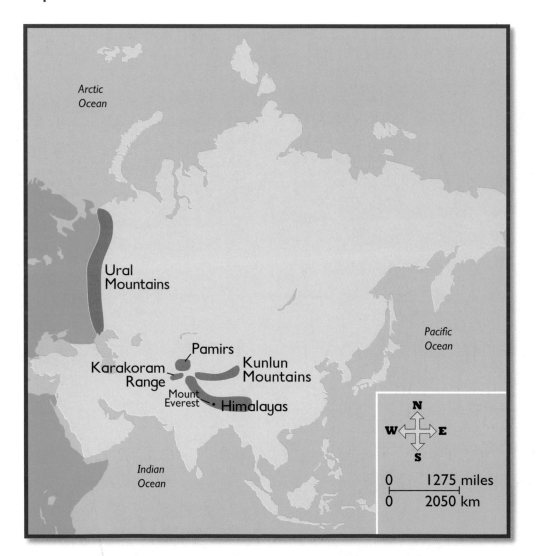

Arctic Ocean

Ural Mountains

Pamirs

Karakoram Range

Kunlun Mountains

Mount Everest

Himalayas

Pacific Ocean

Indian Ocean

N
W   E
S

0   1275 miles
0   2050 km

Mount Everest is the world's tallest mountain. It is the highest place on Earth.

▲ *Mount Everest, in the Himalayas, Nepal*

The Himalayan Mountains are on the **border** between China and Nepal. Parts are also in India and Bhutan. Sir Edmund Hillary and Tenzing Norgay reached the top of Everest in 1953.

Deserts

Much of central Asia is **desert**. The rocky Gobi Desert in China is very hot in summer and cold in winter. People called Mongols live there in circular tents. They are called yurts. They move from place to place.

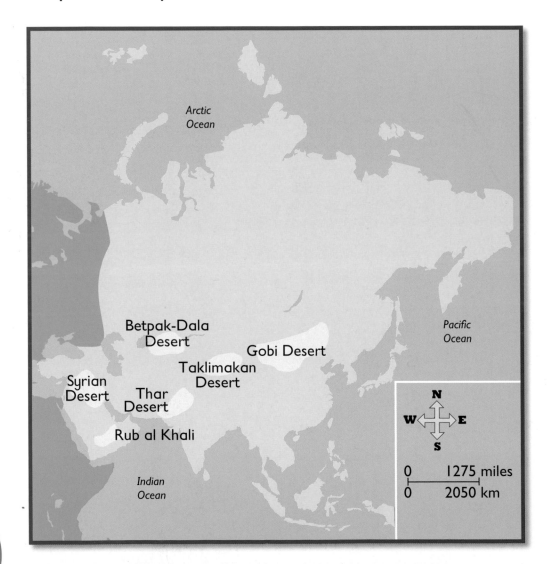

Arctic Ocean

Pacific Ocean

Betpak-Dala Desert

Gobi Desert

Taklimakan Desert

Syrian Desert

Thar Desert

Rub al Khali

Indian Ocean

N
W E
S

0   1275 miles
0   2050 km

▲ *Drilling for oil in Saudi Arabia*

People drill for oil beneath the sandy deserts of southwest Asia. Pipes carry the oil to **ports** on the coast. Large ships, called oil tankers, then take it all over the world.

Rivers

The world's first cities were built by people living near the Tigris and Euphrates rivers. It was easy to grow food in the land there. Farmers sailed along these rivers and **traded** food for other things.

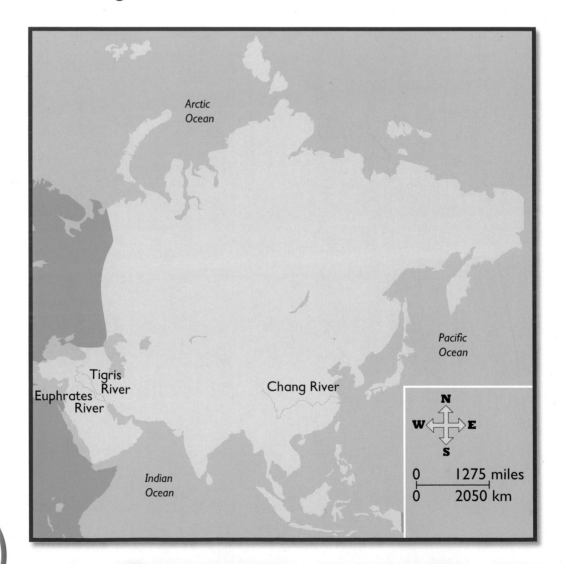

Arctic Ocean

Pacific Ocean

Tigris River

Euphrates River

Chang River

Indian Ocean

N
W E
S

0   1275 miles
0   2050 km

The Chang (or Yangtze) River is the third largest river in the world.

▲ *Chang River, China*

The Chang (or Yangtze) River flows through China for 6,380 kilometres (3,964 miles). People have built huge **dams** on the Chang. The water rushing through these dams is used to make electricity.

Lakes and seas

Asia has many large lakes. The largest is called the Caspian Sea. But it is really the world's biggest **saltwater** lake.

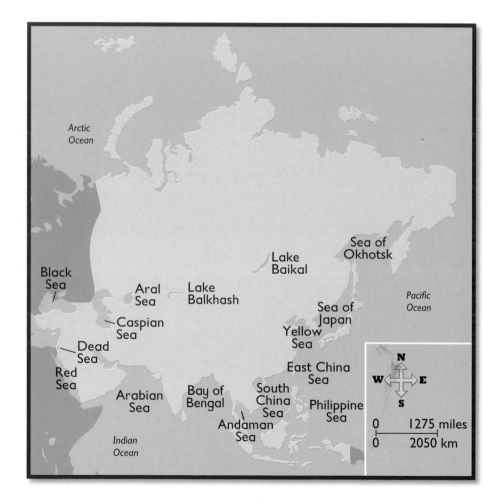

Arctic
Ocean

Sea of
Okhotsk

Lake
Baikal

Black
Sea

Aral
Sea

Lake
Balkhash

Pacific
Ocean

Caspian
Sea

Sea of
Japan

Yellow
Sea

Dead
Sea

East China
Sea

Red
Sea

Arabian
Sea

Bay of
Bengal

South
China
Sea

Philippine
Sea

Andaman
Sea

Indian
Ocean

N
W E
S

0   1275 miles
0   2050 km

▲ *Dead Sea, Israel*

The Dead Sea is also really a lake. It is the lowest lake on Earth. The water in the Dead Sea is so salty that people can float in it very easily.

Plants

Farmers grow rice all over southern Asia. They plant the rice in flooded fields called rice paddies. The islands of Southeast Asia are famous for their spices, such as nutmeg, pepper, and cloves.

Asian farmers grow most of the world's rice, rubber, cotton, and tea.

▲ *Rice paddies, Indonesia*

Bamboo is actually a very fast growing grass.

▲ *Bamboo plants in Indonesia*

Bamboo grows as tall as trees in the forests of China and Southeast Asia. People use the woody bamboo stems to make houses, fishing poles, and **rafts**.

Animals

Giant pandas live in southwest China. They eat bamboo shoots. The Chinese government has set aside special areas of forest where giant pandas can live safely.

Fewer than 1,000 giant pandas now live in the wild.

▲ *Giant panda, China*

▲ *Orangutan, Borneo*

The orangutan is also very rare. This giant ape now only lives in the **rainforests** on the islands of Borneo and Sumatra. People are trying to protect the rainforests and the amazing creatures that live there.

Languages

This map shows the names of some of the countries of Asia. The people of Asia speak many different languages. In India there are 16 **official** languages. But in southwest Asia many people speak Arabic.

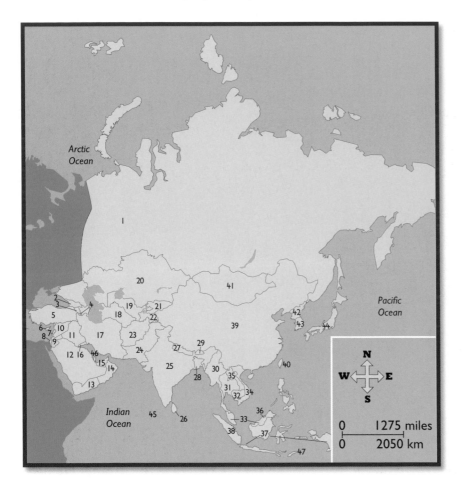

1. Russia	24. Pakistan
2. Georgia	25. India
3. Armenia	26. Sri Lanka
4. Azerbaijan	27. Nepal
5. Turkey	28. Bangladesh
6. Cyprus	29. Bhutan
7. Lebanon	30. Myanmar
8. Israel	31. Thailand
9. Jordan	32. Cambodia
10. Syria	33. Malaysia
11. Iraq	34. Vietnam
12. Saudi Arabia	35. Laos
13. Yemen	36. Brunei
14. Oman	37. Indonesia
15. United Arab Emirates	38. Sumatra
16. Kuwait	39. China
17. Iran	40. Taiwan
18. Turkmenistan	41. Mongolia
19. Uzbekistan	42. North Korea
20. Kazakstan	43. South Korea
21. Kyrgyzstan	44. Japan
22. Tajikistan	45. Maldives
23. Afghanistan	46. Bahrain
	47. East Timor

Children in China have to learn thousands of symbols before they can read and write.

▲ *Girl in school, China*

Many Asian languages have their own alphabets that are used for writing. Some languages have a different symbol for each word. Some Asian writing is read from right to left. Other writing is read from top to bottom.

Cities

Asia has some of the world's biggest cities. Mumbai, in India, is a huge, crowded city. It was built on an island 700 years ago. Mumbai used to be called Bombay. It is famous for its Bollywood film studios. Tokyo is another huge city. It is in Japan.

More people live in Tokyo than in any other city in the world.

▲ Tokyo, Japan

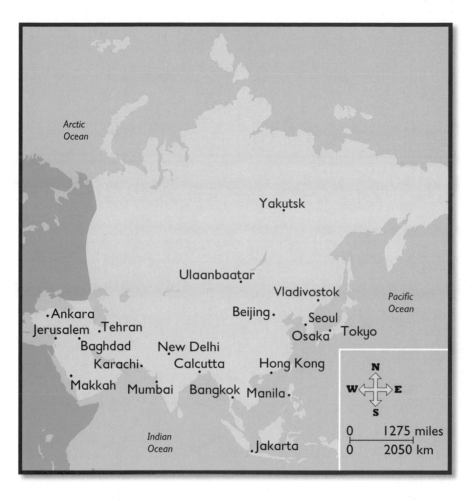

This map shows some of the most important cities in Asia. Makkah, in Saudi Arabia, is an important place for **Muslims**. It is where the **prophet** Mohammed was born. Mohammed started the Muslim religion.

In the country

People called Bedouins live in the **deserts** of western Asia. They sleep in tents and roam through the deserts. They look for places where their animals can eat. Their camels can survive for a long time without drinking water.

▲ *Bedouin, Jordan*

▲ *Floating market, Thailand*

Many Asian farmers live in small villages close to their farms. Some farmers take their **crops** to floating markets. People come to the banks of the river and buy food from the boats.

The Forbidden City is a huge walled palace inside the city of Beijing. It was built 600 years ago by Chinese **emperors**. For 500 years, only the emperor's family and servants were allowed to enter the palace.

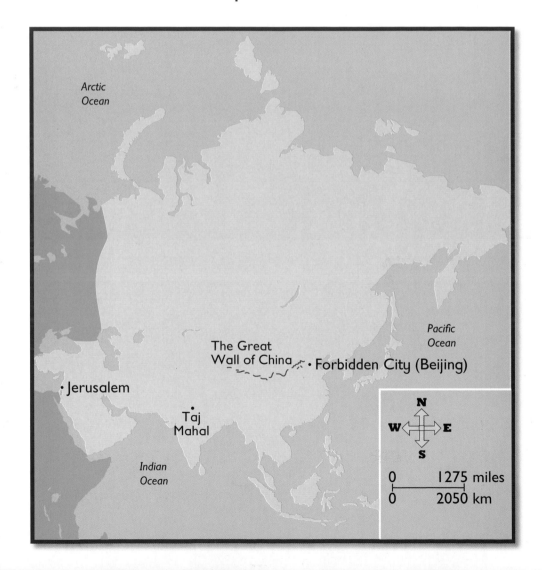

Arctic Ocean

Pacific Ocean

The Great Wall of China • Forbidden City (Beijing)

• Jerusalem

Taj Mahal

Indian Ocean

N
W E
S

0   1275 miles
0   2050 km

The Great Wall of China is so big it can be seen from space.

▲ *Great Wall of China*

The Great Wall of China stretches for 2,250 kilometres (1,400 miles). It was built by the first emperor of China over 2,000 years ago to keep northern warriors out. When soldiers saw an enemy, they lit a fire in their watchtower.

Jerusalem is a holy city for Jews, Christians, and Muslims.

▲ *Jerusalem, Israel*

Inside the city is part of a temple built by a **Jewish** king over 2,000 years ago. Jerusalem also contains the **Christian** Church of the Holy Sepulchre, and the **Muslim** Dome of the Rock. They are all important religious buildings.

The Taj Mahal is a beautiful **tomb** made from white **marble**. A Muslim ruler built it for his wife.

The Taj Mahal took 22 years to complete.

▲ *Taj Mahal, India*

Fast facts

Asia's longest rivers

Name of river	Length in kilometres	Length in miles	Countries	Sea it flows into
Yangtze/ Chang	6,380	3,964	China	East China Sea
Yenisey-Angara	5,550	3,449	Russia, Mongolia	Kara Sea
Huang He (Yellow)	5,463	3,395	China	Bohai Sea

Asia's highest mountains

Name of mountain	Height in metres	Height in feet	Country or region
Everest	8,850	29,035	Nepal/Tibet
K-2	8,611	28,250	Kashmir
Kanchenjunga	8,598	28,208	Nepal/India

Asia record-breakers

Over three billion people live in Asia. That is more than in any other continent.

China has more people than any other country in the world. China's biggest city, Shanghai, has 13.3 million people.

Asia has part of the largest country in the world – Russia. The rest of Russia is in Europe.

Asia has the lowest place on Earth. The Dead Sea is 394 metres below sea level.

All of the world's great religions started in Asia, including Judaism (the **Jewish** religion), Islam, Christianity, Buddhism, Sikhism, and Hinduism.

Glossary

Arctic Circle imaginary line that circles the Earth near the North Pole

border dividing line between one country and another

Christian someone who follows the religion of Christianity, taught by Jesus Christ

climate type of weather a place has

crop plant that is grown for food

dam wall built across a river to control the water

desert hot, dry area with very little rain

emperor ruler of an empire

Equator imaginary circle around the exact middle of the earth

Jewish describes someone who follows Judaism, the religion based on the laws of Moses

marble hard stone that can be polished and used in buildings and statues

Muslim someone who follows the religion of Islam, taught by the prophet Mohammed

official approved by the government

port place where ships come and go

prophet someone who tells about things that will happen in the future

raft simple platform used to move people or things over water

rainforest thick forest that has heavy rain all year round

range line of mountains that are connected to each other

saltwater water that is salty, like the sea

tomb house or room where a dead person is buried

trade buy or sell things

More books to read

My World of Geography: Mountains, Angela Royston
(Heinemann Library, 2004)

Watching Orangutans in Asia, Deborah Underwood
(Heinemann Library, 2006)

We're from India, Vic Parker
(Heinemann Library, 2005)

Index